Ginger
Thinks About Life

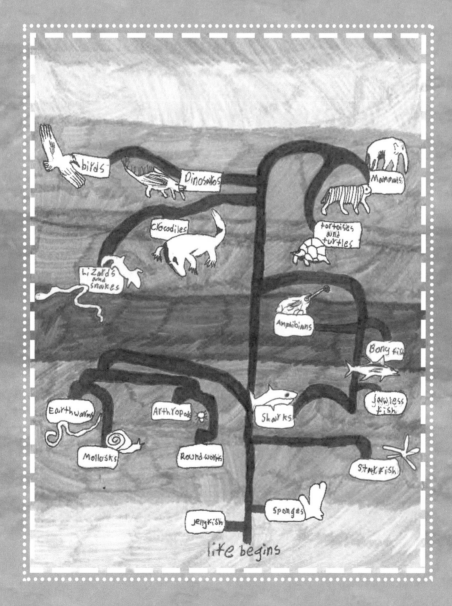

Shannon Oborn

Illustrated by: Emerson Oborn

Order this book online at www.trafford.com
or email orders@trafford.com

Most Trafford titles are also available at major online book retailers.

Trafford
PUBLISHING® www.trafford.com
North America & international
toll-free: 1 888 232 4444 (USA & Canada)
fax: 812 355 4082

Our mission is to efficiently provide the world's finest, most comprehensive book publishing
service, enabling every author to experience success. To find out how to publish your book,
your way, and have it available worldwide, visit us online at www.trafford.com

ISBN: 978-1-4907-9906-3(sc)
978-1-4907-9905-6(e)

Print information available on the last page.

Trafford rev. 12/28/2019

Ginger

Thinks About Life

Shannon Oborn

This is Ginger.

She is angry.

She knows she has to do something.

One day Ginger tells Mother that she wants to run away and live alone. If she lives alone, then she will not be angry at anyone—and no one will be angry at her.

Mother answers that most of God's creatures live alone. They grow up without parents. They make no friends. Once they are adults, they are powerful and rarely angry. But the path to adulthood for a creature without parents is treacherous. Most die.

Ginger thinks about that.

Ginger asks Mother if just the two of them can run away. "We can go to the mountains and grow our own food without school. We will not be angry at anyone, and no one will be angry at us," Ginger says.

Mother answers that many of God's creatures live like this, too. Mothers raise their children alone and protect them. But often boys come and annoy them. Sometimes they seriously hurt them.

Ginger thinks about that.

Ginger asks if Aunt Jo and Cousin Jimmy might like to come with them to the mountains. Then there will be more of them, and they can protect each other.

Mother answers that many of God's creatures live like this, too. Mothers stay with their sisters and friends and raise their children together. "But Ginger," says Mother, "Jimmy will grow up. If he begins to annoy us, then we will not be able to gainsay him."

Ginger thinks about that.

Ginger asks if Coach Austin might want to come with them and Aunt Jo and Cousin Jimmy to the mountains. Coach Austin can ensure that Jimmy is not annoying.

Mother answers slowly. "Many of God's creatures live like this. Mothers and sisters find one adult boy that they know and trust. This special boy protects them from all of the other boys. All the other boys live as bachelors in their own group, away from the the mothers and sisters. If you have sons, they will probably leave the group when they become adults."

Ginger thinks about that.

Ginger says that if Aunt Jo and Cousin Jimmy and Coach Austin were to come with them to the mountains then they could work on manners and respect. Then the boys will not be driven away. Ginger will not be angry at anyone, and no one will be angry at her.

Mother responds carefully. "Many of God's creatures practice manners and respect. There is punishment for those who do not practice manners and respect. But only the bigger individuals can inflict punishment. So manners and respect are given to the bigger ones, and the smaller ones do as they are told."

Ginger thinks about that.

Ginger says that she can stay close to Coach Austin. He will ensure that people treat her with manners and respect. When she finds a boy of her own, then her boy will ensure that she is treated with manners and respect.

Mother nods at Ginger. "This is how the early civilizations started. The girls find one boy to protect them from all of the other boys. The boys fight among themselves for manners and respect. When people lived like this, bigger boys became patrons to smaller boys. The word slavery was invented. All of the ancient civilizations had this word. Most people were slaves."

Ginger thinks about this.

Ginger informs Mother that slavery would make her very angry. Her patron would be angry at her all of the time. "Can we not just have laws that ensure that everyone is treated with manners and respect? Then we do not need patrons, and slavery will not develop?" asks Ginger.

Mother agrees that laws are a first step. "But you must make laws that everyone agrees to, otherwise your community will disappear. When people believe they are slaves, then they do not run away. When people believe they should be treated with manners and respect, then they run away when they believe that they will not be treated with manners and respect."

Ginger thinks about that.

Judges

Legislators

Old Law : ABC
Concerns : DEF
New Law : XYZ

Society

Agent   Construction   teacher   Coach   Haircutter   Firefighter   Police

Doctor   Farmer   Engineer   Bookkeeper   vet   plumber   Electrician

Miner   Trust fund baby   Waiter   Lawyer   Mechanic   Landscaper   Sanitation

Ginger answers, "We will make it easy for everyone to know why a law was written. We will ensure that everyone knows how to change the laws."

Mother grins. "That sounds like school . . ."

Ginger grins back. "Yeah. You're right. But we need to ensure that everyone who is interested in a law can discuss how to make it better. That way, they will not run away."

Mother nods. "That sounds like community. Is it different than what we have now?"

Ginger thinks a moment. "The only difference is that we are not encouraged to talk about laws and how to make them better. Except in school."

Mother smiles. "School is a good place."

Ginger hugs her mother. "I agree."

The Author

Shannon Williams: I love studying our world.

The Illustrator

Emerson Oborn: I love building things.

Printed in the United States
By Bookmasters